Dona Nobis Pacem
(Grant Us Peace)

A Traditional Canon arranged by Deborah Friou

Contents

The harp ensemble has been arranged for three harps. Two harps, taking the first and second or second and third parts, may also play it. I've added a second canon to the ensemble arrangement, which is a variation on the original.

If you wish to simplify the parts, each player may just play the right hand. The first part is written in the bass, the second in the mid range, while the third part is written in the treble end.

The harp solo is a separate arrangement for one harp that includes the three voices of the original canon. All arrangements are in the key of G, have no accidentals, and are playable on folk harp.

It's a lovely piece and the title speaks for itself.

Dona Nobis Pacem

Harp Solo

Arr: Deborah Friou

Traditional

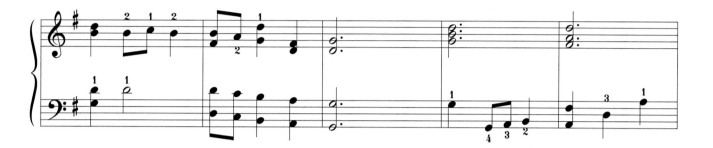

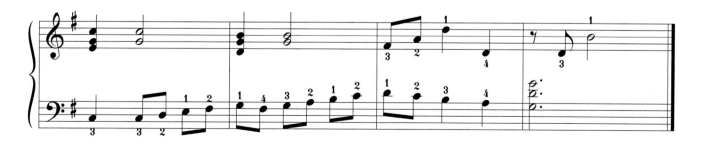

Dona Nobis Pacem
First Harp

Arr: Deborah Friou

Top staff is in bass cleff.

Traditional

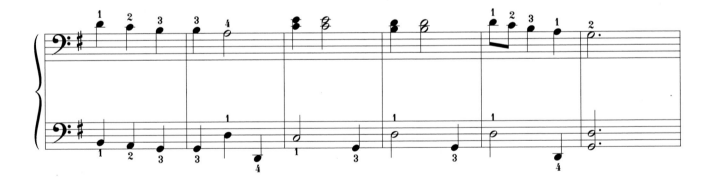

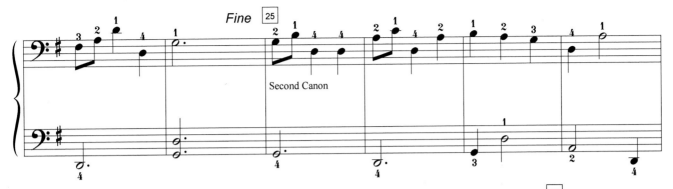

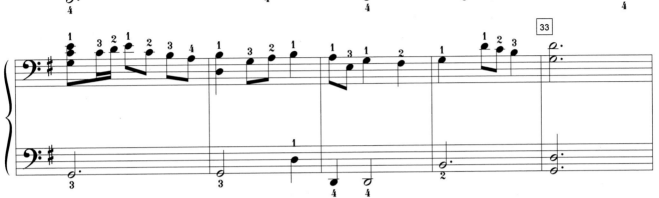

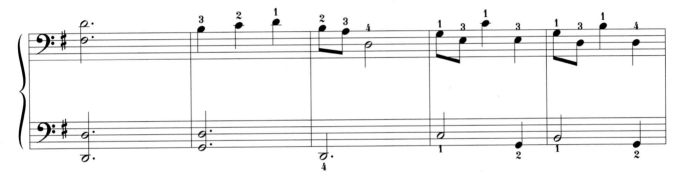

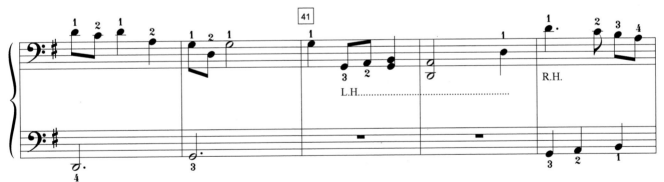

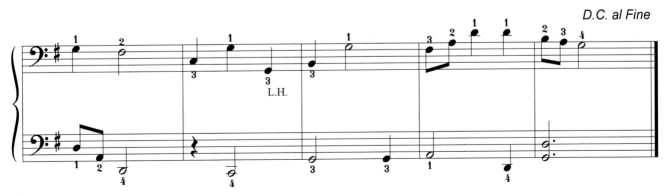

Fine
25
Second Canon
33
41
L.H.
R.H.
L.H.
D.C. al Fine

Dona Nobis Pacem
Second Harp

Arr: Deborah Friou

Traditional

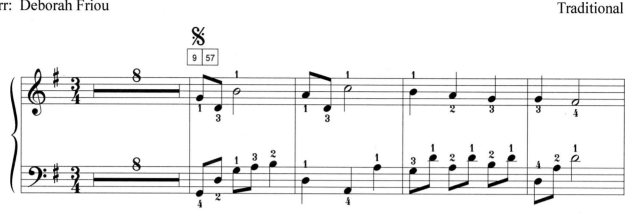

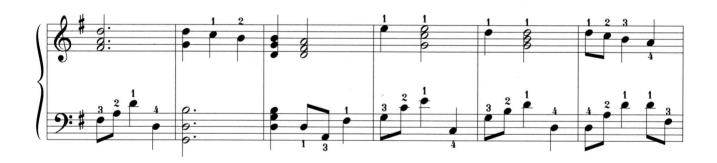

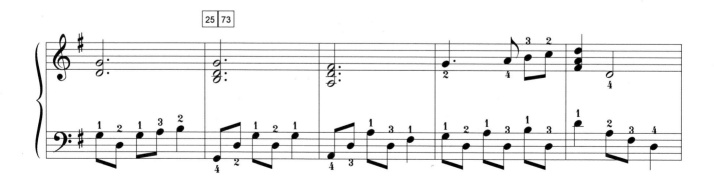

Fine

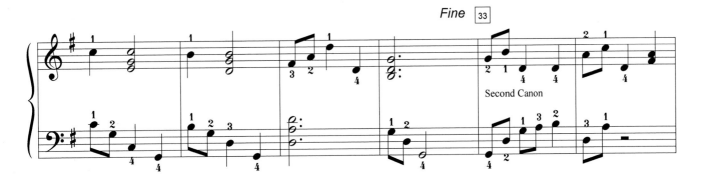

Second Canon

D.S. al Fine

Dona Nobis Pacem

Third Harp

Arr: Deborah Friou
Bottom staff is in treble cleff.

Traditional